Exceptional Customer Service

Retaining your Customers for Life!

(A Survival Skill for Today- Leading to Increased Growth & Profits!)

By
Gerard Assey

Publishing Agency:
Collection Skills
19/18, Palli Arasan Street
Anna Nagar East
Chennai - 600 102

ISBN: 978-81-952564-0-2

Contents

The Importance and Benefits of Providing Exceptional Customer Service

No business today can afford to ignore two very important people -2C's –Your Customer and Your Competitor! The person in front of you is your Customer, and if this person is not treated well, then the person behind you (Your Competitor!) is just waiting to grab him as he drops from your list!
Therefore knowing how to win and retain customers is the single most important business skill that anyone can learn. The business world makes way for the person who brings in the business and the money...and that's the person who wins and keeps customers.
In today's service-oriented economy, excellent service is more than a competitive weapon-it's a survival skill but distressingly only a few organizations are really delighting their customers. Rest assured that if you don't provide this excellent service, someone else would! This therefore has to be the key focus of every organization: to remind themselves that every single person in the organization from the topmost person right to the lowest in rank can effect or have an impact on customers, by the way they treat them and therefore must have the 'hat' of a Customer Service Professional always on. Sales and Service are not to be looked at separate functions-They are two sides of the same coin, both having the same ultimate goal- To satisfy the customer! In today's world it's even more important, where Sales, Marketing, Service and Operations share a common goal: Creating and Retaining Customers. And to create and retain customers we have to combine Good Selling with Good Service.

So what then is this **Exceptional Customer Service or Experience**?
Customer Service or their Experience is the customers' perception of how your company treats them. These perceptions affect their behaviours and build memories and feelings that will drive their loyalty. In other words: if they like you and continue to like you, they are going to do business with you and recommend you to others. And for your customers to like you, you should know them very well to create and deliver personalized experiences that will entice their loyalty. But gaining this in-depth knowledge about customers isn't something that just happens. Organisations will need to work on this with their customers. No doubt, this is well worth the effort.
And it doesn't matter what kind of business you are in – improving the experience for your customers is the key to increasing retention, satisfaction and sales.

Here are some vital data that can help you look at this area of your job on priority

- *For consumers, customer experience will become more important than price and product after 2020.*
- *89% of businesses compete through the level of customer experience they're able to deliver.* -Gartner

- *70% of the customer's journey is dictated by how the customer feels they are being treated.* -McKinsey
- *Businesses that deliver better customer experiences obtain revenues between 4% and 8% above their market.* -Bain & Company
- *55% of customers are willing to spend more money with a company that guarantees them a satisfying experience.* –Think Jar
- *70% of unhappy customers whose problems are resolved are willing to shop with a business again.* -Glance
- *Customer service stats show that new customers cost anywhere between 5 and 25 times more than retaining existing customers.* -Harvard Business Review
- *44% of consumers take their business elsewhere due to a poor experience.* – NewVoiceMedia
- *50% of customers switch brands when their needs are not met.*
- *13% of customers tell 15 people or more if they have a negative experience.* - Esteban Kolsky
- *After one negative experience, 51% of customers will never do business with that company again.* - NewVoiceMedia
- *72% of customers will tell 6 people or more if they have a satisfying experience.* - Esteban Kolsky
- *67% of customers report a bad customer experience as the reason for switching businesses.* -Esteban Kolsky
- *Only 1 in 26 customers will tell a business about their negative experience; the rest simply leave according to customer service facts.* -Esteban Kolsky
- *79% of customers who share their complaints online see their complaints ignored.* -RightNow

And here are some more reasons why customer care is important. These were highlighted in a survey carried out by the CBI (Confederation of British Industry)

- *Only 1 customer in 26 with grounds for complaint actually does so.*
- *Those customers who experience problems tell between 8 and 15 people about the problems.*
- *9 out of 10 people who complain and have a problem that is not dealt with satisfactorily will never buy again from that supplier.*
- *9 out of 10 people who complain and have a problem that is dealt with satisfactorily will buy again or come back.*
- *It costs 5 times more to attract a new customer than to keep an existing one.*

Customers usually don't care about what good you do! On an average when a customer is happy with a product or service, they would generally tell around 7 people, but if the service was bad or if they were disappointed with it, guess how many they would tell on an average?
Without considering the internet, the answer is 38 (just lip service)! But today, with almost everyone in possession of a mobile phone having an internet connection, you do not have to guess the figure!

Bad News certainly travels faster than Good News! You don't have to look far…See today's newspaper headlines, or turn to any news channel or get onto any social media site or platform…What do you get more of? Good news or bad news?
Word-of-mouth advertising is therefore the most powerful form of advertising in the world. And this is what you as a Professional need to keep in mind!

Remember- there are only 3 entrances to any business….
The Front Door!
The Telephone!
The Internet!
…And if either of these are NOT handled well, you have LOST your Customer forever! And in some businesses, this figure can be very high. And remember women can be great INFLUENCERS!
A typical business hears from only 4% of its dissatisfied customers. The other 96% just quietly go away and 91% will never come back. Now that can be a serious financial loss for companies whose people don't know how to treat customers, but a fabulous gain to those that do!
The average business spends six times more to attract new customers than it does to keep old ones. Yet customer loyalty is in most cases worth 10 times the price of a single purchase.
As markets become increasingly competitive, customers can now immediately go elsewhere if they don't get what they want. Continuous overall improvement, gaining competitive edge, increasing market share, raising profits- None of these things is possible, unless businesses can find new ways of maintaining the loyalty of existing customers.

So what then are the benefits of providing Exceptional Service?
Exceptional service will always enable your business to:

- Spend lesser on advertising-Word of mouth works!
- Differentiate itself from the competition
- Improve its image in the eyes of the customer and stakeholders
- Minimize price sensitivity
- Improve profitability
- Increase customer satisfaction and retention
  Build a database of committed customers
- Have a number of advocates or evangelists for your company
- Enhance its reputation
- Ensure products and services are delivered right the very first time
- Improve staff morale;
- Increase employee satisfaction and retention
- Encourage employee participation
- Improve and increase productivity and performance
- Reduce costs
- Create a reputation for being a caring, customer-oriented company
- Build on a list of responsive suppliers

- Foster internal customer/supplier relationships
- Work on bringing about continuous improvements to the operation of the company
- Focus on an improved management team
- Have safer and insured future

EXERCISE: Now try and tailor this to your organization's need by thinking of all the benefits to You, Your Team and Your Organization by providing 'Exceptional Customer Service'

And remember, delivering '**Exceptional Customer Service**' that makes a positive, lasting impression on customers, takes more than courtesy...it's much more! It starts with understanding that Exceptional Customer Service is from the **customer's point of view**. Many organizations spend a lot of time looking inwards and are organized accordingly. The truly customer-centered organization takes time to think through the procedures and systems that work best for the customer. This puts the customer at the very center of the organization.
What you do, how you do it, how well it must be done and proving it can be done again and again...are only the fundamentals and this book: **"Exceptional Customer Service-** Retaining your Customers for Life!" will help you do just that! It will help create a memorable experience for every customer, by meeting expectations and going beyond satisfying their needs- making it easy to do business...thereby making everybody win! The Customer, your Company and the Employees!

How Customers are lost!

In a single year…**Millions** of customers are lost because of poor service!
Clients are LOST
Referrals are LOST
Repeat business is LOST
And…Guess who wins?
Your COMPETITION!

And who do you think are the culprits…
ALL OF US!
We are all unknowingly contributing to these statistics?
"I am new to this department"
"It's not our company's policy to…"
"It's not my job…I handle something else"
"You're not the first to complain about this"
"Sorry you've come to the wrong department"
"I don't see what the problem is…"
"You've come at the wrong time"

Some ways to give your callers a bad experience…

- Being constantly engaged
- Passing them from department to department/ or C.S to C.S personnel
- Making them repeat their story each time you transfer them
- Having them on hold forever, without periodically checking up
- Treating them as a 'nobody'
- Telling them that it's not your job/fault/policy/problem
- Not providing them satisfactory solutions but just 'passing the buck'
- Forgetting to do what you said you would do
- Your tomorrow never comes- Commitments are never kept

A survey on **"Why customers quit"** found the following:

- 3% move away
- 5% develop other friendships
- 9% leave for competitive reasons
- 14% are dissatisfied with the product
- *68% quit because of an* ***attitude of indifference*** *toward the customer by the owner, manager or some employee.*

(With the total showing 99%, you could be wondering what happened to that 1%- Well, because of the death of some of them!)

If you do a little calculation, you will find that a well over 90% is all within your control of turning this around for your organization. Studies show that increasing customer retention rates by just 5% will increase profits anywhere from 25% to 95%, depending on the business you are in.
And remember that your customers won't love you if you give poor service, but your competitors will certainly love you!

Most of the examples cited above on why customers are LOST, have a lot to do only with the human side of dealings. In other words when a customer is disappointed with their expectation of this side (the human behavior) of the service, they CHANGE the service provider without even complaining! The figure below illustrates this well:

Your Customer's Experience

The overall encounter by your customers, that mostly depends on the various 'moments of truth' they experience and the consequences as a result!

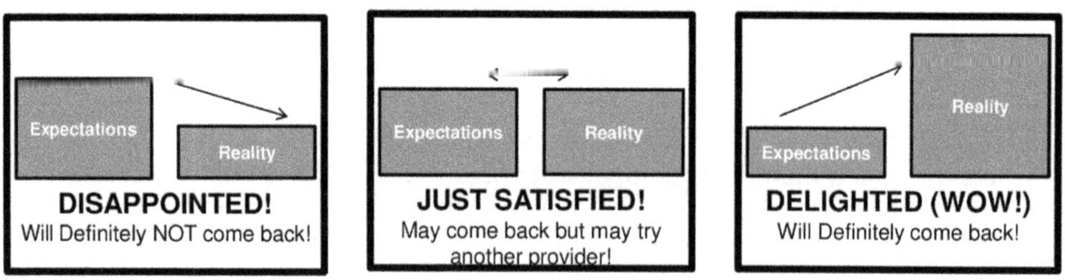

Understanding the Customer Cycle
The figure below shows the typical customer cycle and the 3 groups in a market:

- The Known Market or Your Present Customers,
- The Unknown Market or Your Potential Customers,
- The Lost Customers!

The Customer Cycle

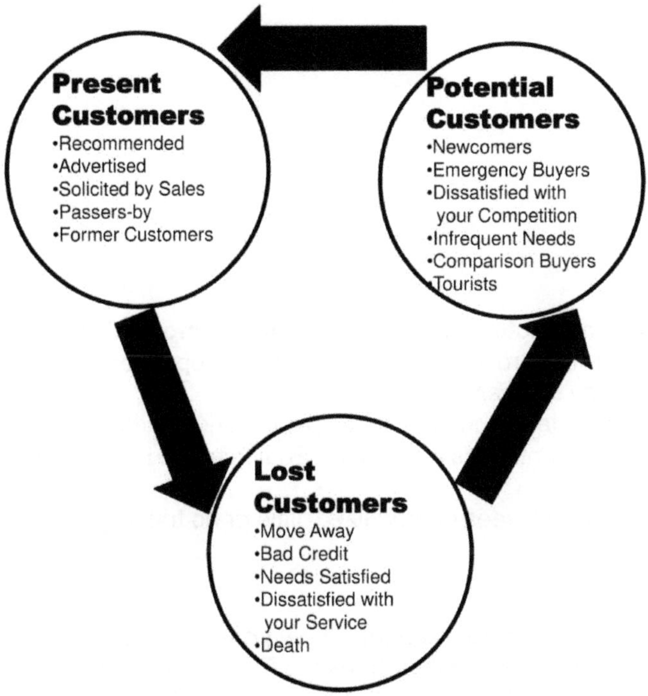

This cycle happens in every business, with almost every business losing customers from a very small fraction of a percentage to a huge percentage, depending on how they have handled them or for other reasons. As fast as a customer is gained, one or more is lost!

...Moreover markets and customers are constantly changing

- Competition is greater than ever.
- There are more choices of products and services
- And more options and avenues to purchase from

So, customers are less loyal in today's marketplace

But imagine if organizations are to focus and work on retaining these lost customers while yet winning those new customers- you could imagine what their business potential and profits would be like!

Here are some internal factors why your customers move away-4 M's!

- **Methods**: Policies/ Procedures, Inadequate/improper complaints system, Lack of flexibility, Values unclear
- **Materials:** Documentation- Too much paperwork, Outdated brochures
- **Machine**/ Equipment: Less machinery/ Equipment to handle customers/ Queries etc
- **Men/** Women: Employees demoralized, little or no training

EXERCISE: ***Now list all possible reasons how your organization could be losing customers due to Internal as well as External Factors and what you/ your team could do to prevent this situation from occurring in future***

How valuable are Customers and what do they really want

Knowing how to win and retain customers is the “SINGLE MOST” important business skill that anyone can learn!
The business world makes way for the person who brings the business and money through the door...the person who <u>wins</u> and <u>retains</u> customers!

Don’t underestimate the valuable of a single customer!
Think for a moment and consider just how valuable customers are. A customer alone makes it possible for you to earn your livelihood in the way you do!
If those customers stop coming in, your organization will not have its business to keep and pay you and its other employees. Just one customer can make or break an organization, depending on how they are served or treated. Today with the internet in the palm of every person’s hand, there is enough bad-mouthing that can be done in a matter of minutes- that can ruin an organizations image and credibility in no time!
The average business spends six times more to attract new customers than it does to keep old ones. Studies have shown that increasing customer retention by just 5% can have a bottom line profit increase of up to 75%. And the ‘Lifetime Value’ of a single customer can be measured in many millions, depending on the type of business. Therefore every customer must be considered both as a powerful tool for word-of-mouth advertising as well as an appreciating asset. Just compare these two: When you build machinery it starts depreciating the very day it is ready. But the well-serviced customer, on the other hand, is an appreciating asset. Every small act on her or his behalf zooms up the chances for repeat business, add-on business and priceless word-of-mouth referral.

What do customers want?
Customers buy experiences!
This starts with their very first contact with you…on phone, person or the internet!
And Remember- there are only 3 entrances to any business….
The Front Door!
The Telephone!
The Internet!
…And if either of these is NOT handled well, you have LOST your Customer forever!

What do your Customers Want!
Various researches have identified a number of factors that seem to influence customers’ decision to remain loyal.

- You keep your commitments/ promises

- You demonstrate your willingness to help: you display a genuine desire to do so
- You and your entire organization inspire confidence
- You treat customers as individuals (All five fingers are not the same!)
- You make it easy for customers to do business with you.(Are you open/ available when they need you; have you tried calling your own telephone lines to see if it is easy getting through; have you tried setting up someone to act as a 'ghost customer' to see how your office treats them)
- All the physical aspects of your product or service give a favorable impression (parking lots, toilets, seating lounges etc)

Know what your callers want!
All callers want C.A.S.H.
Convenience (at theirs, not yours!)
Action (not just lip service!)
Speed (Everyone wants an answer immediately/ early/ now!)
Hassle-free (Not being shunted from one department to another!)

Among B2B decision makers, lack of speed in interactions with their suppliers is the number one pain point, mentioned twice as often as price.

When it comes to making a purchase, 64% of people find customer experience more important than price.

Other Factors:
Convenience-

- Convenient at their time
- Available Help, Fast service
- Delivery as promised
- Phone/Internet Support
- Hassle-Free Returns
- Quick Resolution of Problems

Great People-

- Friendly, Helpful, Courteous, Empathetic, Trustworthy, Knowledgeable, Accurate
- Able to anticipate needs and recommend solutions
- Appropriate Appearance and Demeanor

Only 'EXCEPTIONAL' Customer Service gets noticed

- Are your customers delighted... with your service and do they want to come back to you?
- Can they be easily enticed by a competitor that makes an extra effort to satisfy them?

Exceptional Customer Service is about…

- Treating Customers with **respect** and thinking of them as people the organization might be able to help with its products and services, rather than just 'someone' to be dumped stuff
- Learning what each customer **needs**, and **going beyond** what customer expects
- Being **supportive** and offering help after the sale, and not rejecting requests for help once the money is in
- Developing **life-time relationships** with customers and not just wanting to make a quick sale
- Demonstrating personal credibility (**Adding value and integrity** to each interaction)
- Discovering new ways to **'delight'** those who you serve

EXERCISE: ***From your experience of handling customers in your organisation, what do you think your customers want or expect from you/ your team/ organization?***

YOU are the KEY! Attributes of a Customer Service Professional

What do you need to deliver great customer service?

- A **thorough knowledge** of the **products or services** you offer and the needs of your customers
- A **thorough knowledge** of the **systems and procedures** of your organization and the network of internal customers with whom you work
- **Effective Communication and Professional** Skills
- A Highly Positive **Attitude**

While every business requires **C.A.S.H**. to survive and succeed....Every **C.S. Professional** also needs something to succeed!

Key Attributes of a Customer Service Professional
This chapter will discuss what YOU as a Customer Service Professional will need to specifically have in order for you to achieve your objective and perform in an outstanding manner.
While every business requires CASH to survive and succeed, every Customer Service Professional also requires something in them in order to succeed, which I believe is more valuable than that CASH. This is 'K.A.S.H.' because only when you have this KASH in you, you will be more successful in bringing in the CASH for you and your company- by helping provide 'Exceptional Customer Service resulting in Retaining your Customers for Life'!

So what is this KASH?
Knowledge
Attitude
Skills
Habits
Knowledge is all about your Company, the Products or Services that you offer, the Market and Industry that you operate in, together with knowing who are the other players or your competition that are in this industry. It also involves knowing where you stand against them-your strengths and areas that your competition has an advantage over you, along with being thorough on the rates, polices and regulations in your industry and market.
How effectively are you able to transfer this knowledge to the customer to enable him to deal or decide upon you as a service provider is a skill.
Now there are various types of skill sets that people possess-
Some examples for skills are:
Selling Skills

Time Management
Team Working
Presentation Skills
Ability to present ideas in writing
Strategist- Prepares and Plans
Effective Communication
Negotiation Skills
Now having Knowledge and Skills alone is not enough. There are many sales and customer service personnel that have a great bank of knowledge along with the necessary skills, but yet have been total failures. Reason being they had a lousy attitude or very poor habits that killed a potential sale or the potential in them; that ultimately affected theirs and their organizations credibility
What you are seeing on the pie chart is the mental make-up of a Sales or Customer Service Professional

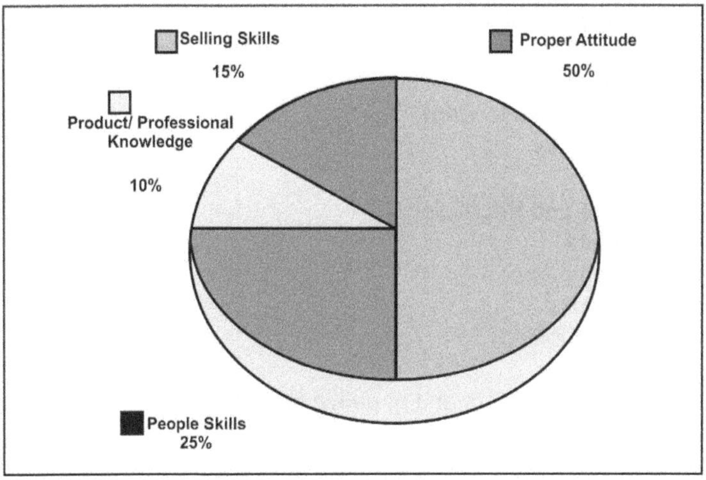

As you will see, 50% has to do with the Attitude, followed by 25% on People Skills. In other words, if you don't have the required knowledge or skills to sell/ service, as you can see, you may be able to still succeed with the right attitude and people skills, because those two account for 75%. Now don't get me wrong, I am not saying that you should not work on your knowledge and skills…Absolutely no!
What I am saying is that given that you have the right attitude coupled with the right people skills, knowledge and selling skills, you don't have to guess where your sales or your service levels would be!
Let us look at this a little differently….Assuming you have the right attitude and people skills, which together comprise of 75% but lack the required knowledge and skills, well then, to me, with the right attitude you can easily learn them. In any case Knowledge and Selling or Customer Handling Skills are teachable, but not Attitude!

Attitude is the outlook or perception towards a given situation, and for a Sales/ CS person this is crucial and foundational! Attitude is made up from our upbringing, environment, exposure etc. It would therefore be extremely difficult or it would take a long time to undo a wrong attitude that has gone in all these years. And for a Sales or Customer Service Professional this is very important- as customers remember the wrong or negative attitude longer. You are the only thing the customer sometimes sees of your company- and this is the impression formed of your entire company- good or bad! It takes a long time to undo this negative feeling about your company in the mind of the customer.

Here are some of the Key Characteristics of Customer Service Personnel who are great at their job:

- Highly Positive attitude
- Enthusiasm
- Communication skills (Ability to communicate clearly/to use positive language)
- Charisma
- Tenacity (Determined/ not giving up)
- Creativity and resourcefulness
- Patience
- Good listening skills
- Capacity and willingness to learn
- Alert and attentiveness
- Multitasking
- Time management and Prioritizing
- Stress management
- Responsible
- Problem solving skills
- Systematic and organized
- A team player
- Resilience-to handle criticism and negative feedback
- Adaptability/ flexibility
- Empathy

EXERCISE: ***From the list above, how many of these attributes do you possess? What can you do to improve or work on attaining the others?***

And all this requires on-going: PRACTICE!

- **P**romptness: Prepared and willing to be of service.
- **R**eliability: Trusting or deserving of complete confidence.
- **A**ccuracy: The ability to observe and act with precision.
- **C**ourtesy: The ability to be gracious, obliging and polite.
- **T**actfulness: The ability to say the right thing without offence.
- **I**nformation: The communication of knowledge or education.
- **C**ompetence: The ability and capacity to carry out a task
- **E**mpathy: Emotional or intellectual identification with the other person.

At this stage it is important to realize that there are **3 A's of Business life**:
Ability, Ambition and **Attitude**
Ability establishes 'what' someone does
Ambition determines 'how much' he does
Attitude 'guarantees how' he does it!

Ability will bring one a pay cheque
Ambition will get him a raise
Attitude alone will lead to success in everything!

Attitude is actually the 'YOU on the job. When ability and ambition in two people are about equal, how does the boss select one over the other for promotion? Here is where Attitude is the deciding factor. Attitude reflects a little plus- that something extra is given willingly though not required.
If you look at the word A-T-T-I-T-U-D-E itself, is it a mere coincidence that "I" comes first and "U" later? If this has any significance, then in trying to understand the attitudes of people, we should first examine ourselves in relation to other people!
Because Attitude is so very important, this is why it is so crucial to fill our minds with the right positive thoughts because our thoughts work into decisions that form our actions and this continued action leads to a habit, which eventually makes up our attitude. Your habits today will become your attitude in the days to come. That's why it is important to check our habits as well. As an example: The habit of late-coming, if not nipped in the early stages can lead it to becoming an attitude, with everything that you undertake being late or delayed!
Here are some examples of positive or right attitude:
Belief
Commitment
Desire
Ability to fail & learn from it
Persistent goals
Self-Motivation
Enthusiasm
Purpose
Self-discipline
Confidence
Creativity
Empathy
Go the extra mile
Self-improvement
Time organization
...and most of all the *PASSION!*

Successful Sales and Customer Service Professionals…

- Understand themselves and how their behavior affects their customers
- Have a positive attitude, which reflects in dedication to getting it right the first time, and commitment to help colleagues to helping their customers
- Know how to adapt their behavior to meet the differing needs of the situation
- A willingness to take responsibility
- Have the confidence to stay calm under pressure

Steps to change your Attitude …

- Become aware of your negative attitude towards yourself, other people and situations and alter your thinking
- Think for yourself and become more constructive
- Keep an open mind

Remember: Changes are always: M.A.D.E…!!!

Developing the Right Sales and Customer Service Attitudes is not something that happens to you-it is something you make happen…and like any change, it is not easy! Here are some steps that can help:

M- Mental Pictures: Visualize who you are, what you want, how will you conduct and carry yourself

A- Affirmations: Add a new self-image by talking positively

D- Daily Successes: Build confidence everyday by looking at your positives rather than negatives

E- Environmental Influences: Surround yourself with positive influencers, read positive stuff, listen and watch positive information etc

You are what you think! To change any habits, you must first change any thoughts, feelings and values!

Changing Bad Habits into Good Ones!

STEP # 1: List your bad habits
STEP # 2: What were the original causes?
STEP # 3: What are the supporting causes?
STEP # 4: Determine a positive habit to replace the bad one.
STEP # 5: Think about the good habit, its benefits and results.
STEP # 6: Take action to develop this habit.
STEP # 7: Daily act upon this habit for reinforcement.
STEP # 8: Reward yourself by noting one of the benefits from your good habit

EXERCISE

- List some of the Key **Attitudes, Skills** and **Habits** that you possess?
- List some of the **Attitudes, Skills** and **Habits** that you lack or are weak in and need to work on?
- By when and what will you do specifically to improve or change the negatives to positives?
- Action Plan

Creating the **'WOW'** Impact!
Exceptional customer service lies not in words, but in your **Attitude** and **Actions**

What is your Attitude towards your customer?
What are your thinking and feeling patterns about the customer?

- *Customers are hard work*
- *Customers exhaust me*
- *Many are a nuisance*
- *Most are very difficult*
- *Quite a few are very demanding*
- *I would prefer to be at home*
- *The fewer the customers, the better*

OR

- *I have the best job in the world*
- *It's fun looking after my customers*
- *I love it when they ask me to help them*
- *It gets me excited to fix difficult problems*
- *I meet many interesting customers*
- *I can't wait to get to work each day*
- *The more the customers the better*

Demonstrating the RIGHT Attitude ...
There are three simple things you can do to be successful in your life and in your business:

- Smile
- Show Interest in other people
- Be a Candle- bring light into the lives around you

How to stand out from the crowd?

- Put your SIGNATURE on everything you do!
- Do it from your heart!
- It's not what you do that matters, but how much love you put in what you do that matters!
- GIVE 100%

Remember: Success is in YOUR Hands

Attitude Impacts Outcome
Steps to change your Attitude...

- Become aware of your negative attitude towards yourself, other people and situations and alter your thinking
- Think for yourself and become more constructive
- Keep an open mind

Here is proof that YOU are the Key to Quality!
Given below are the top characteristics and the percentage of responses that came about from a survey:

- Courteous or polite behavior 21%
- Satisfied 18%
- past experiences 13%
- Recommendation of others 12%
- Promptness 12%
- Price 11%

The traits most displayed by CS personnel whom customers considered to be courteous included: acting promptly; listening carefully; being attentive and understanding; and making "to-the-point" explanations.
The customer respondents added that they liked to be treated with courtesy, friendliness, good manners and kindness. They gave high marks to CS Personnel who were alert, accurate, concerned, and responsible.

This proves again and again that PERSONAL QUALITY is the basis of all other quality and is instrumental in determining an organization's profitability and future!

Conducting and Presenting Yourself as a Customer Service Professional!

A very important part that we would be touching on now is that of how we communicate or the impressions we create even before we could open our mouths.
In a study carried out that I am about to share with you now, you will notice that people place more emphasis on what they SEE rather than on what they HEAR.
So this only tells us that we need to be very careful with our body language and what we are projecting.
According to studies carried out, Communication takes place in 3 forms:

- Your Words
- Your Tone and
- Your Body Language.

Where 55% has to do with your BODY LANGUAGE or what others SEE
7 % has to do with WHAT you say or your words
Whilst 38% has to do with HOW those words are said, which is your Tone or voice modulation
With people going by what they SEE first rather than what they HEAR, it makes it very important for us to therefore project the RIGHT image upfront. That's the impression that has been formed-good or bad! If it is good, then very good for you, but if it is bad, then so sad! Because…now you have double work to undo the wrong impression that has already gone into the mind and to now fill it with the right impression.
They say 90% of lasting impressions are created in the first 90 seconds. That can be really dangerous, but surprisingly that is true! So we have to be very careful, with what are we projecting as soon as someone sees us, because that's what they will remember.
It is also a reason why we tend to remember a song seen on a television set better than when heard through a radio. The same logic applies at a job interview with your resume and the presentation of it! Then at the interview-the interviewer has made up his mind to a great extent as you walk in, even before you have opened your mouth. Your bio-profile or the interview process is only a confirmation of the decision already made in the mind of the interviewer.
Why is Tone next important after Body Language? Simply because you can say a same sentence with a different tone and that can change the entire meaning
Eg; "Mary come here" is a simple sentence. But depending on the right tone this one sentence could turn out as an 'order 'or a 'request'.
Another stronger example: "Hang him not let him go"…could be death or life depending on how it is said. Example: 'Hang him, not let him go'! Or 'Hang him not, let him go'!
Now, if it is face to face, we may be able to save the situation, but when on the phone with the other person not able to see you, it could lead to miscommunication if the right tone is not used.
So as seen, with people going by what they SEE first rather than what they HEAR, it

makes it so very important for us to therefore project the RIGHT image upfront. It basically involves Selling Yourself first!
Before a Customer buys anything or decides to do business with you or the company that you represent, he needs to first be sold on you because you are what he sees about your company to him. Your company could have a several floor building, with several offices all across the globe, but to the customer what he sees in you, is the impression he has formed of your company! Because...90% of lasting impressions are created in the first 90 seconds
So what could you do to improve your image- starting right from the top of your head to the tip of your toes- your hygiene, dressing and grooming, being organized etc. Given below is a suggested checklist to help you project the Right Image!

Checklist- Projecting the Right Image!
Mental- Your mind focused on the customer and not other issues
Physical Aspects like:

- Personal Grooming-Dress for the next level!
- Cleanliness, Breath (floss/ use mouthwash), Hair well groomed, Nails, Body Odor (light deodorant)
- Clean, Pressed/ Proper fit clothes
- Check for stains/ loose buttons
- Pleasant Colors of Clothing
- Polished shoes and in good condition (don't let heels run down)
- Socks (clean without holes, foot deodorant?)
- Clean Spectacles
- Briefcase/ handbag well polished/ in good condition
- Business Cards in pristine, crisp condition (in a holder)
- Good quality pens that write!
- Standing- shoulder square/ sitting- erect
- Sales Kit-Bag-organized /in order/ tidy
- Being Punctual/ Seeking Permission etc
- Mobile phones on silent or off

EXERCISE: ***Develop your own checklist now to suit your specific organization, country and need.*** *(You might like to add on to the list above)*

Hand-shakes and Business Cards
As part of your very first impressions that you are going to create, is also your handshake and the presentation of your business card.

Business Cards
Let us look at the business cards first....
When presenting business cards, they must always be presented face up with the front portion of the card facing towards the customer, and if presenting with one hand as in

most western countries then it must be held by the tip not covering any part of the text on the card.

Some Asian countries present cards with both hands. Whatever be the culture, please ensure the cards are never kept in a wallet as they would tend to get folded or bent at the edges or corner. All cards must be in pristine condition, crisp with no folds, wrinkles or soggy edges.

Whenever presenting the card, make eye contact, with a pleasant smile.

Handshakes…

While it is good to give the other person a firm handshake, it is also important to note that 'firm' should not mean 'bone-crushing' but just comfortable enough for the other person. In other words your handshake should convey 'CARE'!

(Think of: **CAIR**- **C**onfidence, **A**ssurance, **I**nterest, **R**espect)

That is why we recommend that you practice the exact firmness of your handshake first with your own hand. This could be done by taking your left hand out- 4 fingers together and thumb up with the hand facing inwards towards you, as if it is a customers' hand. Now take your right hand the usual way you would use to shake someone's hand and assuming that your left hand is your customers' hand, shake as follows: Web into web first followed by the 4 fingers of your right hand around your left hand, with the thumb finally locking. Basically 3 locks…web into web, 4 fingers around and thumbs interlocked. Since it is your own hand, you will know what amount of firmness to use. Keep practicing till you are comfortable with the right amount of firmness to clasp the other person's hand without it being 'bone-crushing' or the opposite- too limp (a dead fish hand shake!)

You can do this exercise whenever you are free, till you get accustomed to the exact amount of pressure to be used.

Steps to a Professional Customer Service Call

There are 3 Stages of any professional call

- **Pre-Call Preparation**
- During the Call
- Post Call Activities

Stage 1- Pre-Call Preparation:
Script for fixing Appointment!

- Salutation: Good Morning/ Afternoon Mr. So and So!
- This is Jacob-Supervisor from the Customer Service Dept of ABC and Company
- Have I called you at a convenient time?
- I have called you in response to your complaint registered regarding ...
- In order for me to better understand the problem a little more, can I ask you a few questions: Ask Open Questions to unravel problem!
- If understanding of problem is small, such that it can be handled on phone, please suggest!
- Never ask: What is the problem?
- Never say: I just got the complaint from 'so & so'!
- Never say: I had so many calls that I could not meet/ call you earlier!
- Fix Appt accordingly
- Get location/ directions to reach
- Re-confirm time
- Thank customer

Checklist to carry for a day to be better prepared!

- Schedule of Calls for the Day (Territory Mgmt)
- Files/History Case Papers
- Documents pertaining to the accounts for the day
- Business Cards/ID Card
- Pens/ Note pad, Diary
- Anticipate Questions/ Concerns
- Role Play/Rehearse your answers
- Smile/ Enthusiasm
- Fix Appointment
- Business Appointment on time!
- At Customers Place: Introduce Self, Company
- Eye Contact/ Voice/ Right tone -Project Confidence, not arrogance!
- Handshakes
- Giving / Receiving Business Cards
- Respecting Privacy/Putting back things into place
- Your mobile phone on silent or off mode

- Watch your mannerisms!
- Keeping your word!
- Body Language/Posture

Stage 2- During the Call:

- Pre-Call Preparation
- **During the Call**
- Post Call Activities

Imagine that you are a Doctor now!
What do doctors do when you have a headache?

Steps to the Call

- Introduction
- Diagnose (An understanding of the Problem- through effective questioning and listening skills)
- Verify and Confirm the problem
- Reconfirm/ check
- Communicate status to customer
- Provide feedback
- Any other issues?
- Thank and Close Case
- Obtain Testimonials or letter of Satisfaction-Thank Customer!

Learn to wear the RIGHT Hat!
From call to call and even within the same call, Super Customer Service Personnel instinctively know which role to take on:

The type of call	**The Role**
"I'd like to know/have…Please send me…"	**Provider**
"What should I do about…? How can I…?" Which would you…?"	**Advisor**
Distressed caller needing empathy, understanding and reassurance	**Supporter**
Getting the caller out of a challenging situation	**Rescuer**
Solving the caller's problem and complaint	**Problem Solver**

To switch between and perform each of these roles you need to ask questions and listen actively.

Probing Skills-Asking Questions is the Key!
When trying to unravel needs, it must be done in a logical pattern that will bring the customer to a stage of realization.
So the art of uncovering needs requires the use of different types of questions. First let us have an understanding of the different types of questions that we could ask someone. Though there are several types of questions, for the purpose of this exercise let us look at just the 3 most important ones ie;

OPEN Questions
CLOSED Questions
FOLLOW-UP Questions
Depending on what type of answer you want from the other person, either of these questions are used.
Eg; If I asked you: *'Did you have your dinner'?*
Or *'Do you like this training session?'* or *'Are you going home this evening'?*
The only possible answer that you could give me would either be a *'yes'* or a *'no'*
That is why this type of question is called a 'closed question', because the only possible answer would be a one word- with either a *'yes'* or *'no'*
Closed questions usually begin with:
'Are you…'
'Will you…'
'Do you…'
'Would you…'
They are usually not very helpful in starting a conversation and extracting information. However, most sales people are more comfortable asking such questions.
The opposite of 'closed' is the obvious: 'open'. Open questions allow the customer to open up or do the talking and are used to encourage a client to speak freely about a concern or expand on something already raised during the conversation
Always remember this: Open questions generally begin with 5W's and 1 H ie;
Who?
What?
When?
Where?
Why?
How?
And they encourage the other person to open up and speak.
If we were to redo that example again using open questions, they would go something like this: *'What did you have for dinner?' 'How do you feel about this training?' 'What plans do you have for this evening'?*
These questions will certainly not fetch you a *'yes'* or *'no'* like how closed questions do. But they would allow the other person to open up with information which is what you as a customer service person requires.
Shooting out these questions without any logical order would also be inappropriate, as it could be unprofessional, could be irritating at times and most of all cause confusion in the mind of the customer. But if the customer was taken through a logical pattern, it could help lead him or open up to an understanding of his own situation, problem or need- that many times he may not be aware of.

Effective listening involves the use of follow-up questions and they are useful in several ways:

- They show we are interested and encourage the customer to keep talking.
- They increase the quality of the information gained.
- They help us to confirm our understanding of what has been said.

Before we can ask a follow-up question we need to listen to what the customer has said and wait for an appropriate pause in the conversation to ask the question.
Follow-up questions can also take the form of a question asked in response to a statement by the customer. They can reflect the information in the original question by beginning with phrases like:
So you are saying that...?
Does that mean...?
If I understand correctly are you saying that...?
Followed by a summary of what was said by the customer.

Let us see some examples now!
Examples of Open questions:
What exactly do you see the problem as Mr. So and So?
How can I help you solve your problem?

Probing Questions help to dig into or search for details:
"Exactly how did this happen?"
"What steps did you take?"

EXERCISE: ***Now write three examples of your own***

Examples of Closed questions:
Did you receive the letter we sent you on Friday?
Are you happy with the service you have received?

EXERCISE: ***Now write three examples of your own***

Examples of Follow up questions:
What were you told when you rang us?
How quickly were you promised a reply?
In these examples the follow-up questions have been asked in response to the customer saying that he
1) Rang us previously,
2) Was told he would be given a reply

EXERCISE: ***Now write three examples of your own***

EXERCISE: ***List at least 5 Open Questions you will ask the Customer to diagnose the Problem!***

Listening Skills
While the customer talks, you as a customer service person would need to listen attentively.
'People were designed with two ears and one mouth, and that is the ratio in which to use them'!

How to be a good listener?
One of the greatest skills that you as a Customer Service Professional can develop is the skill of listening. The best sales and customer service professionals are the ones that do less talking and more of listening and that is why I believe God gave us two ears and one mouth- so we would do more listening than talking!

Listen Actively

- Focus on the speaker
- Keep an open mind
- Tolerate silence
- Ask open-ended questions
- Repeat the speaker's thoughts
- Listen for facts and key words

To be an "active" listener:

- Suspend judgment, initially
- Avoid distractions; when on the telephone don't carry on side conversations; when face-to-face make eye contact
- Assess what you heard
- Clarify and confirm
- Take notes of key points
- Never use your phone in the customer's premises! It's a big disturbance and bad manners!

Before you respond, assess the information you heard by asking yourself four questions:

- What has he/she told me?
- What can I do with this information?
- What else do I need to know?
- What questions do I still need to ask?

To show you're listening actively:

- Use terms like, 'Go on', Uh huh' and 'mmm'
- Stay tuned in/Watch for non-verbal cues

To show that you have, understood:

- Use, phrases like "I see," "I understand"
- Paraphrase, "So you want me to …"

Clarifying what they said:
In order to more fully understand what is being said we can make it clearer by asking for more detail:

- *You said before you were not satisfied with our service. Can you tell me why?*
- *You mentioned how helpful we had been. In what way?*
- *You said there had been problems in the past. What were they?*

EXERCISE: *Now think of three examples of clarifying statements you might make yourself*

Confirming what they said:
We ask questions to clarify what has been said, but another method is to confirm what has been said by stating it in our own words and asking the other person if our understanding is correct. The method therefore is to

- State our understanding
- Ask for confirmation:
  If I understand correctly, the person you spoke to said they would ring you back within an hour. Is that right?
  What you are saying Mr Frank is that you were promised the paperwork by last week. Is that the case?
  You feel you could have been dealt with more sympathetically. Is that right?

Stage 3- Post Call Activities:

- Pre-Call Preparation
- During the Call
- **Post Call Activities**

Post- Call Activities

- Report Status to Office
- Update History/ File
- Close Complaint in Register/ System
- Obtain after call feedback
- Discuss/ Raise in Service Meeting to prevent from recurring again

Professional Telephone Skills

People who answer the telephone or who work at a help desk are vital members of the company they work for. Their level of performance is invaluable to the overall success of the company. A potential customer's perception of any company is based on how the Help Desk Staff/ Customer Service Personnel handles the initial moment of contact.
If those of us in business were to ask all our customers how they first made contact with us it is highly likely that more than 80% did so by telephone. With most of the business deals half completed on the phone before a face to face contact is made, it is therefore all the more crucial for businesses to ensure that their front office/customer support staff/ receptionists, including secretaries are trained properly in this vital area of telephone answering.
The telephone is such a powerful tool today, but the problem with telephones is that people can't be impressed by the size of your office, the smile on your face, or the clothes you're wearing. They have only two things to go by- your **Attitude** and your **Voice**. People who call your office only once will base 90 percent of what they think of your company on that one call.

Providing Exceptional Service on the Telephone

- The phone's every ring means business in one way or another, so make sure you are treating it like the sales-boosting tool it can be!
- Treat EVERY call importantly
- Every time you make or receive a telephone call at work, you're **representing** your company. The impression you create can be a lasting one so make sure your voice and manner always show you in the best and most professional light.
- When someone feels you're giving him/her personal consideration, they'll have more confidence in you and your company.

Here are some ways that can help you be more professional on the phone:

- Smile! It will show out in your voice
- Picking a ringing phone! 1st, 2nd or 3rd ring?
- Answering your phone: What to say? Greet/ Salutation, your name, department, company name
- Always begin a call by introducing yourself and identifying your company.
- Right tone-Project confidence
- React to the other person's conversation: *"Yes, I see, I agree…"*
- End on a positive note: *(I enjoyed speaking with you Ms. …" or "Thanks so much for your time, Mr… I look forward to meeting you soon.")*
- Hang up after the caller…leaving the receiver quietly down.
- Taking messages: Accuracy/ Spell/ Repeat
- Call back as promised or have someone do so!

- Always ask the caller if he/she would like to hold. Avoid the abrupt phrase *"hold please."*
- Let the caller know how long it will take and ask whether he/she prefers to hold or be called back.
- Update the caller periodically (possibly every 2 minutes). Be as specific as you can be.
- If you are so busy that the call cannot be handled in an efficient manner, give the caller an option of being called back
- Make sure your voice exudes strength and power.
- If someone calls you while you're waiting for your first call to go through, tell your caller you will call him back. *"Good Morning Mr. Jackson, I'm on the other line. May I get back to you in just a few minutes?"* This way, poor Mr. Harry isn't left listening to a dead receiver on the other line. Because Mr. Harry might hang up on you or be unresponsive the next time you call.
- The person you called always has priority.

If you are handling or receiving a call for someone else, then:

- Never demand *"Who is calling?"* Better: *"May I tell him who is calling?"*
- Never tell a caller *"He has left for the day…or at the canteen".* Always: *"He is unavailable at this moment, can I take a message"* or *"May I tell him what you're calling about…maybe I might be able to help!"* (Always show concern!)
  "Ms. XYZ is out at the moment, but she should be back soon. Would you like to hold or may I ask her to return your call"?
  OR
  "Ms. ABC is on another line; would you like to hold?"
- If the caller agrees to hold, remember to return to the line and ask him/her if he/she would like to continue to hold.

When you call others

- Do have a written outline or plan of the topics you want to discuss
- Do leave a brief message if the person does not answer (State your name, reason for the call and the message, telephone number to call back, best time for the return call)
- Do ask if the person has time to talk. If he or she is busy, set up a time to call back
- Do call the person back if you get disconnected.
- Do not eat while on the phone
- Do not talk to others while they are on the phone
- Do not be the first to hang up, and do hang up gently

When others call you:

- Do try to answer the phone within three rings

- Do not say 'Hello'. Use a salutation followed by your name, department, and organization
- If people are calling you at a bad time, do explain and offer to call back
- Do not take multiple calls at one time, keeping people on hold. Do let the voice mail take a message and call back
- Do keep paper and pencil ready

5 Phases of a Call

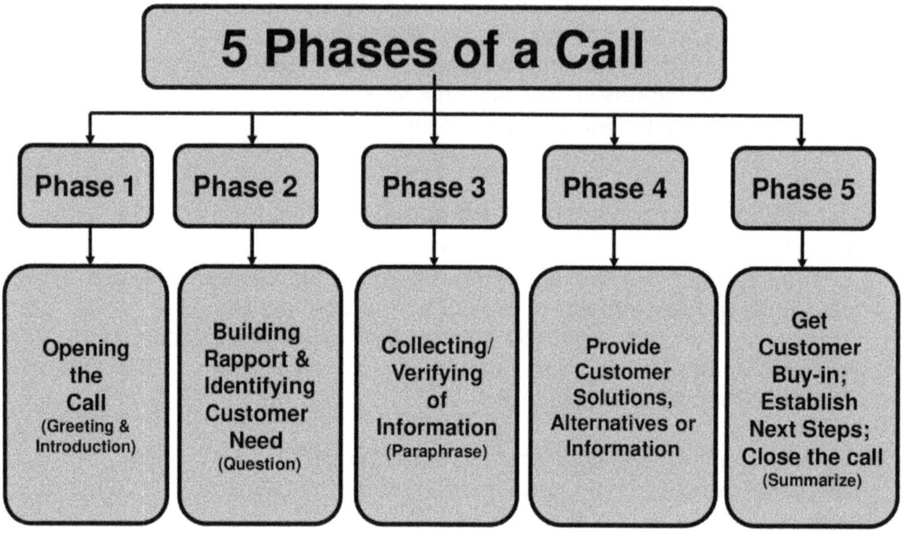

Incoming Calls- Call Structure

The general structure for incoming calls should be:

- Open and introduction
- Ask questions / Listen/ Notes/ Clarify
- Identify the problem
- Recommend a solution
- Commitment to further action
- Close the call

Outgoing Calls-Call Structure

The structure should be:

- Plan and prepare-Keep outline ready
- Open and introduction
- Ask questions/ Listen/ Notes/ Clarify
- Confirm your understanding of the problem

- Recommend a solution
- Commitment to further action
- Close the call

Taking a Message-Establishing the details:
Find out:

- The name of the caller
- Their organization
- Their contact details
- A time when they can be contacted
- The message
- Specific action required
- Repeat this information back to the caller
- Double-check spellings and contact details

EXERCISE! Customer Perceptions!
When customers ring your company with a query or a complaint they have certain expectations that we need to meet.
List 5 things that a customer would expect from a member of staff when ringing your organisation (An example here could be that the customer would expect the query to be dealt with efficiently.

Examples: Some answers you could have given are:

- The query should be dealt with efficiently and immediately.
- The employee should be friendly and helpful.
- The employee should have good product knowledge.
- The caller should not be kept waiting while the problem is solved.
- The caller should not be transferred between different departments.

Finally…Remember that customers form a mental '**PICTURE**' of you from the following:
P-Pitch
I-Inflection
C-Courtesy
T-Tone
U-Understanding
R-Rate
E-Enunciation

Handling Complaints and Irate Customers

What if, every time a customer complained, you looked at it as if a **'Complaint is a Gift',** rather than extra work or them being a 'pain in the neck' to you?
Unfortunately, what often happens is that the front line employees who receive complaints take them personally or blame others. As a result, they over-react and become defensive.
To overcome this kind of reaction, it can help to think of the complaint as a gift- as a genuine desire to solve the problem by someone who has taken the time and the trouble to visit, write or telephone.
It is a chance to set things right! And probably, the <u>only</u> chance! That is why it is like a gift- The customer has given you another opportunity to rectify/ change things. And if you don't change, He will change! (by moving to your competition!)
How many times you would have noticed that all that the customer really wanted when he complained was an acknowledgement of the problem, an apology, an explanation or a solution to the problem…And most times the solution offered could have been just a hearing out!

By complaining, customers are giving you several opportunities like:

- Helping you find out what you need to do to improve your systems and procedures
- See your service from the customer's point of view and try to make changes- He is the spokesperson for the many others that do not open up.
- Identify areas where your company could train your staff.
- Help you identify new products/ services/ opportunities which the market may require from you. (This is free information that you can get!)
- When customers share their story, they're not just sharing pain points. They're actually teaching you how to make your product, service, and business better.

So what do customers look for when they complain?

A customer who has taken the trouble to complain to an organization expects:

- **Someone to listen** actively to the complaint, to be sympathetic and to take responsibility for its resolution
- To **deal** with **one or two** people only- not to be shunted from person to person or department to department.
- And a **quick** solution.

By encouraging your customers to complain, you help resolve their problems quickly and effectively:

- You keep existing customers
- You develop your relationships with them.

- Those customers are likely to win you more customers because they will go and tell friends and relatives how impressed they were with you.
- The original complaint itself becomes unimportant!
- You now have another brand ambassador

But…why most customers do not complain?
Here are several reasons that might sound familiar to what could be happening in your organization:

- *I tried complaining in the past- but nothing really happened*
- *I don't think anyone will listen to me- they seemed to be only after my money*
- *Nobody is willing to take responsibility over my complaint- but just keep passing me from one person to another*
- *I don't think my complaint will be welcome*
- *Whenever I make a complaint, I am looked at and treated with suspicion and doubt- always treating me like a criminal and subjected to interrogation*
- *I am not treated politely. They are very rude when I complain, but treat me on top of the world when getting my order*
- *I don't know who or how to go about complaining- no access provided on their website or elsewhere*
- *If I send a complaint in writing, it takes so long if they do reply, but most times they never even get back.*
- *Complaining is more trouble than going elsewhere*
- *Their websites and other promotional material talk so much of how customer focused they seem, but all this is only in empty words- they really don't mean it!*

What are some of the Key Pre-requisites for handling complaints?

- Top Management to have the 'Right Attitude' (as this attitude very soon percolates down- knowing what is done, is what the organization rewards)
- The 'Right Attitude' and Behavior of people receiving and handling the complaint
- Strong Systems, Policies and Procedures- friendly and fast (Not just smiles!)

What if you put yourself in your customer's shoes?
You cannot truly understand your customer's experience or how your customer feels without putting yourself in his shoes. Learn to deploy empathy and awareness to the other person's needs. Knowing your customer's wants and needs is one thing. Understanding "the why" behind their decisions is another. Try asking yourself-If the same incident happened to you:

- *What would your initial reaction be?*
- *What would you think and feel? Why?*
- *What questions do they have right now that would really clarify the problem we solve, and a need for its solution?*
- *What would you expect from the service provider as being fair to you?*
- *What would I most want in the long run by solving the problem?*

- *What would it require to make you happy- to continue to be dealing with the service provider, by being their 'goodwill' representative and talking only well of them*

By putting yourself in your customer's shoes it will help you understand the customer's needs and expectations and place you in a better position to be able to handle the complaint efficiently

Here are a few 'Golden Rules' for processing complaints:

- Always thank the customer, explaining why you appreciate the complaint raised
- Apologize for the mistake/ error/ slipup
- Take ownership to resolve the problem
- Commit to do something about it immediately
- Verify that your proposed solution will address their needs
- Work on correcting/ rectifying the mistake/ error immediately
- Check to see for the customer's satisfaction
- Work on putting a system in place to prevent such mistakes from occurring in future

Handling Complaints requires RESPONSIBILITY!

- Where errors/ mistakes/ slipups have occurred, resist the urge to argue, to defend, justify or to provide excuses
- Admit mistakes and apologize sincerely- you are the representative of everybody in the organization- you are the brand ambassador.
- Even if the request or the problem sounds familiar, don't jump to conclusions until you have gathered all the facts
- Offer to follow-up personally; give your name and number. Customers want consistency in their dealings with the company, and prefer not to explain their situation again to someone new.
- Look for solutions, not obstacles or excuses!

A few DON'TS to keep in mind!

- Do not appear disinterested.
- Do not lose your temper or show your exasperate on with the situation to the customer.
- Do not let the customer know this is as common complaint if you have heard the complaint many times before.
- Do not appear inflexible. Saying, "well, its company policy', or, 'We can't do that', will aggravate the customer.
- Do not blame other people. The customer is not interested in your internal politics; he or she needs a solution to their problem now.
- Don't get defensive or argue about complaints. Be empathetic.

- Don't make the customer repeat their complaint. If you have to transfer their complaint, either in person or on the phone, show the customer you have been listening by summarizing the problem for your colleague.
- Don't leave the customers waiting in the office or holding on the phone too long. Keep them informed. Offer to call back if you don't have the information.
- Never tell them what you can't do for them. Emphasize what you **can** do.

Key steps to handling complaints:

- **Thank the customer:** The fact that the customer has come or called to complain, means that they are giving your organization a chance to rectify things. You have another opportunity to turn this customer as a well-wisher. He could have gone away quietly- but he has given your organization another chance- grab it and use it to turn the customer around.
- **Listen and stay calm**: Aim to diffuse the customer's feelings and clarify the exact nature of the problem.
- **Don't justify, argue, make excuses, interrupt or pass the buck**: Just stick to the facts, keep off what happened in the past and focus on what is going to happen now.
- **Sympathize:** This means sympathizing with the fact that the person has a problem, not accepting any blame as you are currently hearing only one side of the story (theirs).
- **Ask probing questions to verify facts:** This will give you more detailed information about the specific complaint and allow you to see a way through to a possible solution to the problem
- **Check back your understanding:** Reconfirm or paraphrase what you heard.
- **Agree a course of action and timeframe**: It is essential to find a solution which is satisfactory for the customer and from your organization's point of view.
- **Check that the course of action is carried out:** If you agree with the customer that something will happen by a certain date, you must check that it has in fact happened. If it hasn't, you must take action to avoid making the problem even more serious.
- **Check for the satisfaction of the customer**
- **Thank the customer**
- **Work on setting your system** in order to ensure such mistakes or lapses are not repeated

Delight your customers, while resolving complaints!

You choice of words are to be 'POSITIVE' to demonstrate empathy!

- Never say: *"I don't know"* (Instead say, *"That's a good question, Let me just find out for you"*, or offer to get back, after finding the answer…')
- Never say: "I/we can't do that" (Instead use positive statements, such as, *"This is what I/we can do."*)
- Never say: *"You will have to"* (Instead say, *"you may need to"*, or *"I need you to please.."* or *"Here's how we can help you"*)

- Instead of *"Sorry to keep you waiting"* you could say, *"Thank you for waiting/holding".*

Turn Negative to Positive!
Some useful phrases you can use:

"I'll be glad to…"
"What would you consider right or fair?"
"I'm sorry you feel that way"
"Would you be willing to…?"
"Thank you for drawing this to my attention."

Dealing with IRATE Customers
What sort of Customers do you honestly like or prefer?
'Nice Customers' (the ones that do not shout or get agitated)
or
The 'Barking' Ones' (the emotional/ irate ones)?

Most people love these so called 'nice customers'- the ones that do not shout, and avoid the 'barking one'. But it's these so called 'nice customers' that are dangerous- they will slip away to your competition, without even telling you.
The so called 'barking ones' are those that are giving you another chance to change- grab this opportunity. And these few are the representatives or spokespeople of the many that are slipping away, without providing you any feedback. So welcome them with open arms!

How to deal with IRATE Customers

- Give the customer space to let off steam before you try to steer them towards a discussion
- Don't take it personally, and always be calm
- If the customer is abusive and you can't steer the conversation onto how you can solve the problem, seek help from your supervisor
- If the customer won't calm down and they've caught you unprepared, agree to look into the problem and tell them when you'll call or e-mail them

Always remember that: An Angry Customer…May have 4 F's that could be bothering them!
Fitness: They may have a health problem
Family: They may have a spouse/ children/ other family problem
Finance: They may have a money problem
Firm: They may have a job problem (boss/colleague/ other)
And they may just be taking that out on you!
Take it seriously – not personally.

When handling a highly emotional or irate customer, think of the acronym: '**LEAPS**'

- **L**isten: Allow the customer to vent out all their feelings. Do not interrupt or argue
- **E**mpathize: Acknowledge the person's feelings ('*I understand how you feel about this…I would have felt the same too*')
- **A**pologize, even if the problem is not your fault (You could say, *'I am really sorry this has happened...'*, and really mean it)
- **P** (Be) **P**ositive all through the conversation by focusing on the facts and directing your thoughts to your future actions, not the past.
- **S**olve: Suggest or generate solutions that you can both agree on and/or ask what you can do to help: If reasonable do it/if not, find a compromise.

Steps to handle an Angry Customer

Dealing with an angry customer is an opportunity to learn, and an opportunity to turn a negative situation into a positive customer experience. How you react to an angry customer can make or break the perception the customer has about your organization. Instead of backing away or avoiding an angry customer, use this opportunity to improve your product or service, and to work on building a better relationship with your customer. This is a great opportunity you have to solidify your relationship.

Here are a few key steps to keep in mind by taking responsibility when dealing with irate or dissatisfied customers – and turning them around to be your mouthpiece and ambassadors for your organization.

- Listen all the way out. Make sure the customer has told you everything. Don't interrupt.
- Ask open questions to understand their problem better, and to find out what it will take to help them – the way they want to be helped.
- Tell them you understand how they feel (This is powerful- try it!)
- Empathize with them. (Cite a similar incident or tell them that it makes you upset too) Empathy doesn't necessarily mean agreeing with the customer. It means you truly understand how they feel. Comfort them.
- Maintain a calm tone of voice all through the conversation
- Use the customer's name in your conversation
- Agree with them, if at all possible. (Never argue or get angry.)
- Take notes and confirm back that everything has been covered, and they have said all they want/need to say.
- Be an ambassador for your company. Tell the customer you will personally handle it
- Don't blame others or look for a scope goat. Admit you (and or your organization) were wrong and take responsibility for correcting it.
- Apologize for the problem they're having. Acknowledging the mistake and letting the customer know you're really sorry will go a long way. Be thorough in your apology.

- Don't pass the buck. *"It's not my job."..."I thought she said this..." "He's not there right now."*... or *"Someone else handles that,"* are responses that are never right or acceptable to the customer.
- Avoid negative speech- Tell them what you can do, not what you cannot!
- Don't take it personally- but do take it seriously
- Respond immediately. When something goes wrong, people want (and expect) it to be fixed immediately. The customer wants it now- not at your time. Don't we all want it that way when we are customers ourselves!
- Find some common ground other than the problem. (Try to establish some rapport.)
- If you have the gift for humor, use it if possible. It is a very powerful tool as making people laugh puts them at ease.
- Work out all possible solutions, communicate, and agree upon the best solution. Give the customer choices if possible.
- Follow this up by confirming in writing if necessary. Tell them what you plan to do... and DO IT!
- Make a follow-up call after the situation is resolved. Check to see if they are totally satisfied
- Get a letter if you can. Resolving a problem in a favorable and positive way strengthens respect, builds character, and establishes a solid base for long-term relationships. Tell the customer you would appreciate a sentence or two about how the situation was resolved.
- Ask yourself: "What have I learned, and what can I do to prevent this situation from happening again? Do I need to make any changes?" Where?

Processing written complaints

Here are a few key points to keep in mind when processing written complaints:

- The customers complaint should ideally be acknowledged with a personal letter immediately
- Always thank the customer- clearly demonstrating that the customer is important and explaining why you appreciate the complaint that was raised.
- A recognition of the customer's right to complain
- An apology for the mistake/ error/ slipup
- A commitment from your end to do something about it immediately
- Work on correcting/ rectifying the mistake/ error immediately
- A final reply sent to the customer on the action taken
- Check to see for the customer's total satisfaction
- A copy of letter to concerned department internally to work on putting a system in place to prevent such mistakes from occurring in future

LETTERS- COMPLAINTS

When handling complaints show 'CUSTOMERS concern:

- **C**oncern for clients

- **U**rgency
- **S**pecific facts
- **T**imetabled actions
- **O**ptions to resolve
- **M**ailed confirmation
- **E**mpathy for them
- **R**espect

Always use customer's feedback to:

- Improve overall systems and procedures
- Eliminate product defects or work on improvisation
- Improve the attitude and behavior of your customer service personnel and others in touch with customers through training!
- Focus the organization more on customer's needs
- Set higher performance standards

Steps to Improving your Service-Setting Standards

Every time a customer calls or you call a customer, you have an opportunity and a choice.
What choice are you making?
Excellent service is not what you believe it to be, but it's what your customer perceives it to be. And tells others!
And what better person to ask than your very customer that is using your product or service. Sadly, many organizations spend several hours locked in board rooms discussing how to make this person (the customer and end user) happy, without ever including the customer in the discussion.
And you can simply and easily get this golden knowledge and information by asking customers these two powerful questions:

- *How are we doing?*
- *How can we get better?*

Finding the answer to these two questions will tell you:

- The customer's perception of your quality of service
- What to do in order to increase that perception

But most organizations never want to do this as it would mean pricking and disturbing a bee's hive!

Setting Standards of Performance
Here are the key steps to improving your overall system and setting standards of Performance
1. Find out what your customers want: Eg; through questionnaires, surveys, visiting customers, telephonic conversations, you or someone reliable actually experiencing your products or services first hand and providing genuine feedback.
Customer satisfaction surveys are most crucial as they can help you to check if you are providing the service expected by your end users. They help you keep a high level of customer satisfaction that can be a strong predictor of customer retention, loyalty, and product repurchase by quickly responding to negative experiences.

So here are some of the specific questions you could ask your customers about the quality of your service that you could use to tailor to your own organizations need:

- *How well do we deliver what we promise?*
- *How often do we do things right the first time?*
- *How often do we do things right on time?*
- *How quickly do we respond to your requests?*
- *How satisfied are you with the process of getting your problem resolved?*
- *How much effort did you personally have to put in to have your request handled?*
- *How did this effort compare to your expectations?*

- *How responsive have we been to your questions or concerns about our products/service?*
- *How accessible are we when you need to contact us?*
- *How helpful and polite are we?*
- *How well do we speak your language?*
- *How well do we listen to you?*
- *What did you feel about the time taken by our customer service personnel to solve your issue?*
- *Did they have the required knowledge?*
- *What was the wait time for your query to be answered? Did it meet your expectations?*
- *What is your overall satisfaction with our customer service personnel?*
- *How would you rate the qualities of our customer service representative?*
- *What would best describe your experience with our customer service personnel?*
- *How hard do you think we work at keeping you a satisfied customer?*
- *How much confidence do you have in our products or services?*
- *How well does our product meet your needs?*
- *How well do we understand and try to meet your special needs and requests?*
- *Overall, how would you rate the appearance of our facilities, products, communications, and people?*
- *Overall, how would you rate the quality of our service?*
- *Overall, how would you rate the quality of (our competitor's service?)*
- *How willing would you be to buy from us again?*
- *Considering your overall experience, how likely would you be to recommend us to a friend or a colleague?*
- *On a scale from 0 to 10, how likely are you to recommend our company to a friend or colleague?*
- *To what extent do you agree with the following statement: The company made it easy for me to handle my issue*
- *What would you say to someone who asked for feedback about us?*
- *How easy was it to navigate our website?*
- *What are the most important areas of service we are missing?*
- *If you could change just one thing about our service, what would it be?*

2. Translate information gathered to defined standards: Eg; Resolve every complaint received within 24 hours, return call within an hour for at least 98% of customers
3. Communicate this information to the entire workforce: top to bottom: so there is consistency at all levels and all follow without doubt
4. Measure Success: Check for reduction in number of complaints, errors etc
5. Continue using Measurement Results: By Analyzing, identifying problem and communicating to all by following the above 4 steps

Setting Standards of Performance

Find what customers want	Through questionnaires, visiting customers, telephonic conversations, actually experiencing your products or services first hand
Translate information gathered to defined standards	Resolve every complaint received within 24 hours, return call within an hour for at least 98% of customers
Communicate information to workforce	Top to bottom: so there is consistency at all levels and all follow without doubt
Measure Success	Check for reduction in number of complaints, errors etc
Continue using Measurement Results	By Analyzing, identifying problem and communicating to all

Your Company Policy!
After you've set up your internal standards and policies, remember to NEVER tell a customer that *'IT'S OUR POLICY TO DO IT THIS WAY*!' Customers hate to hear this! Remember that your customer didn't call to get a lesson on your company policy. They called to get help! And if you don't give it to them, they will call or go to someone else!

Your company's policy was written to tell you and your department what you cannot do- it is a guideline for you and your colleagues and NOT a lecture for your customers. So instead of the word 'policy' you can try the phrase *'in order to be fair to everyone*!'

Finally...Always use your customer's feedback to:

- Improve overall systems
- Eliminate product defects or work on improvisation
- Improve the attitude and behavior of your customer service personnel and others in touch with customers through training!
- Focus the organization more on customer's needs
- Set higher performance standards
- Keep constantly reviewing your policies and procedures

EXERCISE! Standards of Performance

Think of your specific department. You are going to identify situations where you give and receive customer service and identify standards of performance that relate to the service you give to your internal and external customers. Remember, to be effective they should be:

- Achievable
- Measurable
- Ambitious
- Relevant
- Time bound

Begin the exercise by listing 10 situations in your day to day work you have contact with customers (internal or external).

For Example:

In the customer service department we will set, as our standard, the maximum number of rings allowed before a telephone is answered to be three. This will be reviewed weekly by Mr. ABC

Other Examples:

A customer calling in with a query
A report being produced for another department
A customer order being processed

Now work out your own Standards…

Start with Step 1 by picking at least 15 questions to make up your questionnaire that you can have administered to your customers. (Pick at least 3 questions from each different area related to product, service, behavior, facilities, response etc) and then move onwards to doing step 2 from the results received.

Learning to Manage Stress for continued Success

Your job as a Customer Service Professional can sometimes seem to be a very thankless job- catering to demands and being yelled at for things that are out of your control. Though dealing with customers can most times be really pleasant with a fulfilling experience, yet sometimes it can get very difficult when you are pressed from all sides. Nobody calls customer service department to offer praise; they usually call because they have a complaint, and they can often be angry and unreasonable at such times. Customer service professionals, who are often the voice behind their brands, feel that stress more than other professions.
Moreover, there are other types of pressures that sales and service personnel experience. The figure shows the four types that can affect one

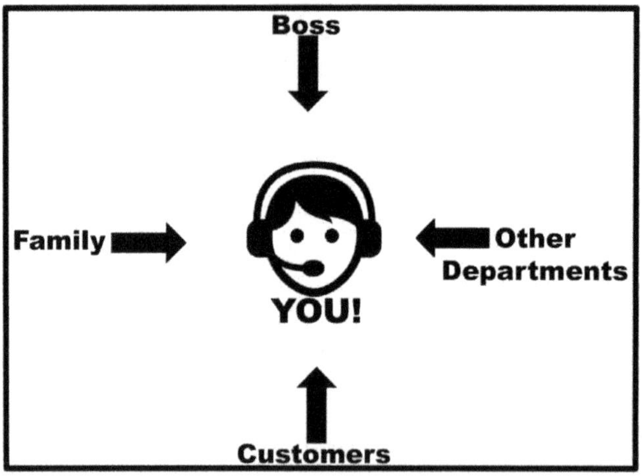

- Boss
- Customers
- Other Departments: operations/ manufacturing/ colleagues/ office politics
- Family

Symptoms of stress: what to look out for?
- Headache
- Stomach upset

- Aching muscles
- Restlessness when sleeping
- Fatigue
- Loss of appetite
- Irritability
- Low morale

Thus, stress in this setting is all too common, and it can have some serious repercussions on an individual, if not handled properly. Learning to manage stress therefore is essential for a successful and upward career.

Here are a few things that you could do, to help you stay above it:

- Get to know what makes you feel stressed out by understanding your body's stress signals.
- Don't be a sponge for the customer's anger: Don't take it personally. Change your perspective: view problems at work as a challenge and nothing more
- Remember: When customers are frustrated, their behavior is a reaction to unmet expectations and needs- behind this could be the 4F's (see in one of the earlier chapters) that are surfacing now through this incident
- Talk it out with your friends/colleagues
- After handling a difficult customer, take a moment or two to unwind; Don't rush straight into the next angry customer
- Breathe very slowly and deeply for at least a minute while a customer is venting- deep breaths can help calm your nerves.
- As a CS Professional, you may always be sitting at a desk all day, with not much physical movement or activity. You could during your breaks take long walks to help you ease that stress. Get away from your desk for short periods of time.
- Maintain a healthy work/life balance: Find time to focus on yourself and family
- Prioritize your activities for the day to maintain control
- Exercise, eat right, and sleep well
- Listen to good music
- Always take time to relax
- Keep a diary of 'Laughs' that you can always get back to, to cheer you up!

A Final Word!

Most of the strategies or steps in this book should have hopefully given you some fresh ideas for approaching a customer and providing them with Exceptional Customer Service, but they are certainly not a cure-all. Your product, service and most of all the attitude and behavior of everyone in your organization will do most of the work in keeping customers loyal, for there are no shortcuts. Again, there are many books and customer retention strategies, but this one thing is for sure that will be very noticeable-standing out loud and clear in all of them –that there are NO shortcuts.
You will eventually realise that providing 'Exceptional Customer Care or Service' results in high levels of customer satisfaction leading to long-term `buying' relationships between suppliers and customers, with customers always coming back!
Your current customer base is the best asset your organization can have. Customers already know your brand, they know your products, and they appreciate your service. So focusing your team's time, efforts and energy on improving the experience for this group as opposed to only being in search of new customers can be a powerful way to skyrocket revenues for your organization.

And here's the **Final Key** that is summed up in one word: **C.A.R.E:**
Customers
Are
Really
Everything!

So go ahead and give your customers that Exceptional CARE and see your business and profits zoom up!

About the Author

Gerard Assey is a Graduate in Economics, a PGD in Management (HRD) and holds a Doctorate in Leadership. Gerard holds several International Qualifications in Sales, Debt Collection, Training & Teaching, and is a 'Fellow' of the prestigious 'Institute of Sales & Marketing Management'-UK, a Certified NLP Practitioner, a 'Certified Trainer', an 'Accredited Management Teacher-Behavioral Sciences', a 'Certified Competency Facilitator' and a 'Certified Management Consultant'- (the International credentials of a professional management consultant, awarded in accordance with global standards of the ICMCI); He is also a Member of the 'National Association of Sales Professionals' & a Member of the 'Institute of Management Consultants' backed with several years experience in varied industries, both in India and Overseas. He also holds an 'Etiquette Consultant' Certification from the USA (by Sue Fox, Author of Best Seller: 'Business Etiquette for Dummies'. She has trained some of the top celebrities' world over). He was also a recipient of a scholarship for extensive training in Japan on 'Corporate Management for India'.

Gerard Assey is 'Founder & Chief Corporate Trainer' of the Group: **'Citius, Altius, Fortius Unlimited'**- an organization that **celebrated 19 years of Glorious Service** in **2020**, focusing on 3 Core Competencies: People. Performance. Profit; in functional areas of Sales & Marketing, HR & Organizational Development, covering Recruitment, Training & Consultancy!

Having managed organizations with large Sales Forces in India and Overseas, his specialization is naturally in the area of Sales Training (All levels with Presentation, Negotiation, Key/ Strategic Accounts Management & Managerial Skills for all sectors), Bid Proposal/ Capture Planning/ Management Trainings, Retail Sales, Customer Service & Customer Retention Programs, Training for Prevention & Collection of Debt, Self & Personal Development Programs (Time Management, Teamwork & Team Building, Business Etiquette & Personal Grooming, Leadership & Managerial Skills, People Management Skills, Train-the-Trainer etc), including preparation of Custom-designed Business Manuals for Internal (HR, Induction, and Sales etc) & External use (Instruction, User Manuals).

Gerard has successfully conducted over 5500 Trainings & Workshops all across India, Middle East, Africa, Europe & S.E. Asia. Besides public programs conducted regularly, both in India & Overseas, he has some of the top names as clients whom he services from Single Owners to large Public & Government undertakings, covering all sectors, for their in-house needs.

His website: www.CollectionSkills.com is the only one in this part of the world to be featured in the 'Collections & Credit Risk Magazine-USA' under 'Who's Who in Training'. Gerard is author of 22 books (as on March 2021),
A few of the secular books being:

1. Bite-sized Bits on Commonsense Management
2. Heart to Heart on Life's Principles'
3. How to become a Successful Manager
4. The Sales Professionals' Master Workbook of S.Y.S.T.E.M.S
5. The Professional Business Email Etiquette Handbook & Guide
6. The Professional Business Video-Conferencing Etiquette Handbook & Guide
7. Professional Presentation Skills

...And some of his most recent Christian Books being:

1. 'A Bouquet of Praises for My KING',
2. Christian Jokes for the Serious Religious' Folks!
3. Jesus Healed You!
4. Praise24Ever!
5. The 5G Network of GOD
6. Building Faith over F.E.A.R-**F**ACE **E**VERYTHING **A**ND **R**ISE with **JESUS**
7. Hebrew and Greek Praise and Worship Words
8. Godly Mothers' and Grandmothers' Bible Story time for Kids
9. Miracles of JESUS in Pictures
10. Raise your Praise All 365 Days: (SON Rise Praises from Genesis to Revelation to begin each day!)
11. Thanking GOD with an Attitude of Gratitude
12. Meditating on the Attributes of GOD
13. Puppet Scripts

Besides regularly contributing to business & trade journals, including international ones such as the 'Creative Training Techniques' and the 'Sales News' of the U.S.A, He is also a member of several prestigious bodies & trade associations, having participated in many Conferences & Workshops in India & Overseas.

Prior to his last assignment of leading &managing a large MNC as head, Gerard had a 3-year stint in the Middle East as a Consultant with a leading British Consultancy Firm. As the past 'Official Country Representative' for the International Business Award- 'THE STEVIES'-(the business world's own Oscar) for about 4 years- he ensured a few Indian companies that qualify for the same every year!

Gerard can be contacted at:
E: mail: training@Sales-Training.in
training@CollectionSkills.com

Websites:
www.Sales-Training.in
www.EtiquetteWorks.in
www.CollectionSkills.com

www.RetailSalesTraining.in
www.SalesTrainingIndia.com
www.ManualPreparation.com
www.TrainingWithPuppets.com
www.FirstContactAcademy.com
www.Skills2Win-Just4Teens.com
www.SalesAndMarketingRecruiter.com

www.ingramcontent.com/pod-product-compliance
Ingram Content Group UK Ltd.
Pitfield, Milton Keynes, MK11 3LW, UK
UKHW021410190726
13845UKWH00028B/1005